Dogs

Wendy Boorer

Octopus Books

Contents

First published in 1975 by
Octopus Books Limited
59 Grosvenor Street, London W1

© 1975 Octopus Books Limited

ISBN 0 7064 0436 X

Produced by Mandarin Publishers Limited
14 Westlands Road, Quarry Bay, Hong Kong

Printed in Hong Kong

Companions of man

There is no other animal that becomes quite such a member of the family as the pet dog. This companionship has always been appreciated, although all of us might not want to go as far as the first-century Greek historian Arrian, who said 'Nothing is so helpful for the dog as a warm, soft bed. It is best of all if they can sleep with a person, because it makes them more human, and because they rejoice in the company of human beings.'

Rejoicing in the company of humans is perhaps the dog's greatest asset. When the family was a larger unit, everyone had a chance of finding someone with the time to give them affection, offer them sympathy and listen to their troubles. With smaller families and less leisure, loneliness is an ever-present, ever-growing problem and the uncritical flattery of the pet dog often affords some sort of consolation for a largely indifferent world. Talking to the dog may be a poor substitute for talking to another human being, but it is certainly better than talking to oneself. This companionship is often under-estimated, for the loyal adulation of the family pet can be of great value to the child who is feeling unjustly misunderstood or who is consumed with jealousy.

Pet dogs fulfil many functions for their owners and have the advantage that they can be ignored when they are not needed. You do not have to be on your best behaviour with the dog. You can take out your anger and frustration on it and it will be glad to see you just the same. Many people like the dependency of keeping a dog. The urge to feed and care for someone or something is a very fundamental one and a dog will never become independent or be ungrateful. To pet and fondle an animal can be a sensual tactile pleasure and the dog will make no demands in return. The pet dog fulfils different needs for different owners and with the stresses of modern life these needs seem to grow more rather than less.

Unfortunately all owners do not consider the dog's needs as well as their own. Primarily the dog is a social animal which should not be left alone every day when the family goes out to work. A bored and lonely dog can be both noisy and destructive, so if you have to be out all the time it is better to choose some other pet which is less demanding in this respect. A dog needs a diet suited to its own needs, and this means a fairly high proportion of that expensive commodity, meat. A surprising number of owners buy a dog they cannot afford to feed. A dog also needs daily exercise and this depends on the owner's time and energy. No dog should be allowed to roam. The town stray fouls the pavements and causes traffic accidents. The country dog on the loose also causes accidents and there is always the danger that it will end up chasing someone else's stock on someone else's land and get shot. If it seems impossible to keep your dog at home, except when it is being exercised by someone, then, again, choose some less demanding pet. The dog needs to be kept clean and well groomed and someone has got to be responsible for this. If you are attracted by the glamour of a long-coated breed, remember that ten minutes of regular daily attention is going to be needed to preserve that eye-catching appearance. Finally the dog is going to need a certain amount of training, both for your sake and the sake of the community.

You may want to keep a dog for any number of reasons but the people around you may not be animal lovers. They may be indifferent or hostile but their rights should be respected. Your dog should not be allowed to foul the pavements or footpaths. It should not be allowed to bark continually, nor to frighten people by boisterous or aggressive behaviour. A well-trained dog will never be a nuisance in ways like this.

Your choice of dog should be dictated by the amount of space you have, the amount of time you are willing to spend and the amount of money you can spare to meet the weekly food bill. But even within this framework there is an enormous variety of breeds and types from which to choose. You can suit your own personal taste in the matter of your pet's looks and, to a certain extent, in the matter of its temperament. This is one of the main advantages the pure-bred animal has over the mongrel. If you choose a pedigree puppy, you will know the size to which it will grow and how it will look when adult. You will even have some idea of the type of temperament to expect. With a mongrel all this is much more of a gamble. The initial cost of a pure-bred animal will be more, but this difference in cost spread over the ten years or so of a dog's life is little enough to pay for a certain pride in ownership. With a pedigree dog you may even be tempted into the show ring and discover a new and fascinating world. You may also find that training your dog gives you so much satisfaction that you will want to enter obedience competitions. Either of these activities will increase your pride and pleasure and deepen the bond between dog and owner. Whatever your personal preference in looks and character, you should be able to find it somewhere among the hundred or so different breeds available. From then on what you make of the companionship of your dog is up to you.

The family dog
All dogs need plenty of daily exercise, and the larger the dog the more exercise it will need. Taking the dog with you for a walk when you go shopping ensures that it has regular exercise, but you must remember to keep it under control and not let it foul the pavements.

Mongrels like these often make excellent family pets and loyal companions.

Australian Terrier *Left*
The Australian Terrier is one of
the smallest of the working terriers
and one of the few terrier breeds
not created by British fanciers.
First shown in Melbourne in 1885,
the Australian Terrier is a compact,
low-to-the-ground, very active dog
with the gameness necessary to
tackle all the smaller inhabitants of
the bush. Valued more today
because it is a sensible-sized dog
for those living in flats and small
maisonettes, its spirit and air of
assurance make it an excellent
housedog. It has never been among
the most popular of breeds, but
its workmanlike qualities assure it
of a steady future.

Boston Terrier *Top right*
The Boston Terrier, produced in
the 1870s in the town it was named
after, is popular all over the world,
being described by some as 'the
perfect American gentleman'. A
clean-cut little dog, it should ideally
be brindle in colour with the all-
important white markings evenly
placed. The Boston Terrier was
originally bred for pit fighting and
was probably developed from
crossing Bulldogs and Bull Terriers.
The aggressive spirit is no longer
apparent in the breed, although
they are still well able to take care
of themselves if necessary.

Brussels Griffon *Bottom right*
The Brussels Griffon is a toy dog
which is small in size but big in
personality. The hansom cab
drivers of Brussels had small
rough-haired dogs which rode
importantly on the front seat of the
hansom when their masters were
working and caught the rats in the
stable in their off-duty hours. The
gamin charm of these dogs
attracted attention and, modified
by crossing with various other
breeds, the Brussels Griffon was
born. They are sturdy little dogs,
built like cobs, and full of a sense
of their own importance. There are
two varieties of coat, rough and
smooth.

Cavalier King Charles Spaniel *Left*
The Cavalier King Charles Spaniel is one of the most popular toy dogs in Great Britain, possibly because it combines a small compact size with a distinctly sporting character. This breed was re-created in the 1920s due to the enthusiasm of an American. He offered British breeders a prize if they could produce the type of toy spaniel seen in contemporary portraits of Charles II. This led to the rebirth of the Cavalier, a breed which ironically is scarcely known in the States. Princess Margaret's patronage of the breed has further increased its popularity.

Chow Chow *Top right*
The Chow Chow presents an aloof leonine appearance and is a dignified dog, loyal to its owner but with little interest in other people. The characteristics of the breed include the rather scowling face, a bluish-black tongue which is unique in dogdom, and an almost straight hindleg which causes the Chow's unusual stilted gait. These same breed features were described by an English naturalist in the eighteenth century and had obviously been hallmarks of the Chow for many centuries. Chinese in origin, the Chow has served many roles in its homeland, among them draught dog, gundog and even table delicacy.

Maltese *Bottom right*
The Maltese, looking like a scrap of fluff when a pup and an advertisement for a washing powder when older, is a sweet-tempered, spirited little dog with a great sense of fun. Its recorded history is a long one and, as the pet of people of culture and wealth, it has been shown on Greek tiles and vases, mentioned by early natural history writers and painted by everyone from Reynolds to Landseer. Although tiny, it is a volatile and hardy dog whose only disadvantage seems to be a coat that needs frequent attention if it is to be seen at its best.

French Bulldog *Top left*
There was great controversy over the French Bulldog when it was first brought to England from France in the late 1890s. Die-hards maintained that the Bulldog was so British a breed that even the thought of a French Bulldog was impossible. However, not only did they exist, they also flourished, particularly in America. It was in the States that the very distinctive upright bat ear was securely established as a breed characteristic. Robust and active, the French Bulldog is a much less exaggerated shape than its English counterpart. The smooth coat can be brindle, fawn or pied.

Yorkshire Terrier *Bottom left*
This diminutive Yorkshire Terrier will grow up to 8 ins (20 cm) tall and weigh up to 7 lb (3 kg). The short fluffy coat will grow to floor length, and be a dark steel blue and tan colour with a fine silky texture. If the dog is a show dog, its owner will be constantly preoccupied with protecting its coat. A pet 'Yorkie' often leads a life more suited to its natural character for, although many lead very pampered lives, they are spirited dogs which like to rush about in true terrier fashion, if given half a chance. The Yorkshire Terrier is the most popular toy dog in Britain.

St Bernard *Right*
The St Bernard, one of the ten most popular breeds in the United States, is another canine giant. These dogs are associated with legendary feats of rescue, finding and guiding to safety travellers lost in the snowdrifts of the St Bernard Pass across the Alps. Although mountain rescues still take place, the work is now done by the lighter and more versatile German Shepherd. The benevolent and kindly disposition of the St Bernard, plus its impressive size, ensures the dog a host of admirers.

King Charles Spaniel *Left*
The King Charles Spaniel or English Toy Spaniel is a short-faced toy breed which was more popular in late Victorian times than it is today. This breed has always been divided into four different colour varieties, each distinct enough to have its own name and history. These are the Prince Charles, which is a tricolour of white, black and tan; the Ruby, a chestnut red; the Blenheim, white and red; and the black and tan. The popularity of the larger Cavalier has quite eclipsed the King Charles, which is in danger of disappearing altogether.

Bedlington Terrier *Top right*
The Bedlington Terrier is possibly one of the oldest terrier breeds, and has been known in the Northumberland district of Britain since the early 1800s. Often called the Gypsy Dog, the Bedlington was the poacher's partner, for the breed combined the vermin-killing instincts of the terrier with the speed of a hound like the whippet. Trimming emphasizes the dog's distinctive outline, and its lamb-like appearance is heightened by the unique flaxen texture of the coat and the fact that most Bedlingtons are blue in colour, although liver and sandy are also acceptable.

Pug *Bottom right*
The Pug first came to Britain from Holland. It was very fashionable in the mid-Victorian era when every lady of note felt she had to own one. The earliest Pugs were fawn with a black mask, and the first all-black Pug was not shown until 1886. When the adjective 'Victorian' became synonymous with 'old-fashioned', the Pug also fell out of favour. Today there is a revival and the Pug once again has a host of admirers. They are thickset, compact dogs which do not require coddling. They are alert and playful but a watch needs to be kept on their waistline as a fat Pug is an abomination.

Bulldog *Left*

The British Bulldog is the national symbol of tenacity and courage, both of which were needed in the days when the dog was used for bull-baiting. Once bull-baiting became illegal, the dog changed both its shape and its character. Now the massive scowling head masks a gentle and affectionate nature and its cumbersome shape implies that the Bulldog prefers a comfortable, amiable way of life to the rigours of its past existence. Both modern Bulldogs and modern bulls have become muscle-bound leviathans, very different from the days when they were pitted against each other.

Shih Tzu *Top right*

The Shih Tzu is a flat-faced breed which originated in the Far East, in this case Tibet. These fascinating little dogs were kept as watchdogs and behave with the dignified good manners appropriate to such an important position as guardian to the household. The long dense coat and the heavily plumed tail can be any colour, but a white blaze on the forehead and a white tail tip are prized. As their coat reaches the ground and they move with great energy, they have been referred to as 'canine hovercraft'.

Dalmatian *Bottom right*

The Dalmatian must have a claim as the dog with the most nicknames, being affectionately known as the 'plum pudding dog', the 'spotted Dick' and the 'fire-house dog'. The distinctive spots make it an easily recognized dog and since the success of the Disney film, *101 Dalmatians*, the breed has been more widely kept than ever. The Dalmatian first became popular, however, as a carriage dog. As well as destroying stable rats, the 'Dally' trotted out with the horses and, as a smart spotted accessory, lent a final air of distinction to a gentleman's equipage.

Chinese Crested *Top left*
The hairless dogs have always been amongst the rarest and most bizarre of breeds. The only one to have made any real headway is the Chinese Crested, which is now exhibited regularly in Britain. Except for the plume of hair on the tail and the crest on the head, the dog is naked. The skin colour varies, but it is usually mottled like the bark of a plane tree. The reason for the hairlessness is not known and, without the protection afforded by a coat of hair, the Chinese Crested has to be guarded against sunburn as well as extremes of cold.

Chihuahua *Bottom left*
The smallest dog in the world is the Chihuahua, which can weigh as little as 1 lb (453 g), although 4-5 lb (1.81-2.27 kg) is a more realistic weight. This little dog, in spite of its size, is both robust and hardy. The breed originally came from Mexico, caught the fancy of the American public and is now one of the most popular breeds in the world. The smooth-coated Chihuahua has always been the favourite but the long-coated dog is rapidly catching up.

Papillon *Top right*
The Papillon is a member of the dwarf spaniel family. The large fringed ears, carried obliquely, suggest the wings of a butterfly, as the French name implies, and a well-defined white blaze on the face represents the body of the insect. A rarer type with drop ears (called 'phalene' or 'moth') shows more clearly the relationship to toy spaniels. These dogs were favourites at the French court where their small size and high spirits were much valued.

Boxer *Bottom right*
It seems odd that so popular and well known a dog as the Boxer should have such a comparatively short history. The breed is a German one, developed from dogs of the bulldog and mastiff types which were used for bull-baiting and dogfighting. Energy and courage are characteristics still possessed by the modern Boxer, a breed which makes a devoted companion and guard. The Boxer was one of the first breeds used for police work in Germany but did not become popular in Britain or America until the late 1940s.

Italian Greyhound *Left*
The Italian Greyhound is the bantamweight in the great grey-hound family. We do not really know how the breed was miniaturized, only that it probably happened more than two thousand years ago. These are ornamental pet dogs, with an air of luxury and refinement, and they prefer the comfort of a carpeted apartment to the rigours of the chase. They have always been valued in aristocratic circles and have appeared in the background of many pictures painted throughout the centuries by the world's most famous portrait painters.

Pekinese *Top right*
The Pekinese is one of the most popular toy dogs in the world. The romantic story of how four of these dogs were found by British troops during the looting of the Imperial Palace in Peking in 1860 caught the public's fancy. This, however, would not have been enough. It was the character of a dog which combined dignity with exasperating stubbornness, and comical charm with playfulness, that ensured its popularity with so many people. Pekinese are tough and sturdy animals with profuse coats which can be in any shade.

Lhasa Apso *Bottom right*
The Lhasa Apso, also known as the Tibetan Apso, reached the Western world in the 1930s. Valued as watchdogs, the Apsos were sometimes given to foreign diplomats by the Dalai Lama and in this way they became known in the outside world. As with all long-haired breeds, the puppies are enchantingly fluffy. When considering such a dog as a pet, however, it is important to remember the problems associated with such a heavily coated adult. Two hours a week would be the minimum needed to keep it in order.

Gun dogs

Many of the present-day breeds of gun dog are descended from the sporting dogs used from medieval times to the advent of the sporting gun. Hawking was one of the favourite pastimes throughout Europe for centuries and dogs were employed to find and flush the game for the waiting hawks circling overhead. Today falconry is very much a minority sport but dogs still perform the same function for the hunter with his gun. There is no reason to suppose that in medieval times any special breed was used. All that was needed was an active dog with a good nose.

Confusingly, early writers call all the types of sporting dogs by the name of 'spaniel'. We know, however, that different kinds of dogs were used for different functions. Springing spaniels found birds like partridge and quail and flushed them into nets. Setting spaniels or 'couchers' also used their noses to find the coveys but, instead of flushing the birds, they showed they had found game by freezing into position with head held low, one forefoot raised and tail rigidly held out behind. The aim was to try and pin the birds to the ground long enough for a movable net to be drawn over both birds and dog. In the work of the springing spaniel we can see the forerunners of the present spaniel breeds, while the setting spaniels foreshadow setters and pointers.

The earliest guns, or 'fowling peeces', were inaccurate and did not have any great range, so they took a long time to come into general use. Nor was there any feeling that it was unsporting to shoot at sitting birds. Indeed so unreliable were the guns that sportsmen were advised never to fire unless it was at a group of stationary birds. As the range was so short, there was no need for a dog to collect the birds for they fell almost at the hunter's feet.

With the arrival of the breach-loading gun, the sport of shooting really began and pointers and setters came into their own. These are dogs which locate their quarry by windborne scent. They quarter the ground, ranging far ahead of the line of guns, and are lightly built, fast dogs of great stamina, which may be required to gallop across moorland all day. It was on the grouse moors of Yorkshire and Scotland that the work of pointers and setters was first seen at its best. When the dogs scent game, they freeze in the classical pose of a pointing dog, indicating the position of the birds, and try to keep them pinned down until the guns arrive. Only then, on command, do the dogs creep forward until the birds lose their nerve and fly upward, presenting a target. At the sound of the shot the dogs drop down and remain still until once more waved on to quarter the ground.

The breaking-up of large estates and the consequent curtailment of moorland used solely for shooting means that the pointer and setter are no longer pre-eminent as working gun dogs in Britain, but they are still used very extensively in the States where field trials are enormously popular.

As sporting guns improved, the increased velocity meant that birds flying high overhead often fell a long way ahead of the guns. This led to the development of the retrieving breeds whose job was simply and solely to fetch back dead and wounded game. As injured birds will run great distances, retrievers had to have good noses so that they could track birds down. At first any dog that would fetch and carry game was called a 'retriever', but by 1880 all the retrieving breeds that we know today were established.

Spaniels also find and flush game but they work within the range of the gun and flush birds within that range. They flush game out of cover and are used for working through undergrowth and hedgerows, searching fields of root crops or stubble. Because this type of shooting is within the reach of the majority of shooting men, the working spaniel, in practice the English Springer, is the most widely used of modern gun dogs.

Spaniels are also expected to retrieve but they are not so versatile as the final group of gun dogs, which might be described as 'all-purpose' gun dogs. These are mainly continental breeds which are expected to find and point their birds, flush them on command and then retrieve them when they have been shot.

There is a great deal of public interest in the work of gun dogs and field trials are held in which the work of the dogs is tested competitively. These are particularly popular in America where separate trials are run for pointers and setters, for the all-purpose breeds and for retrievers. Because of the numbers involved and the enthusiasm shown, many of the conditions are artificial and the game is planted. This is in contrast to British field trials which take place under natural conditions. Although this means that these trials approximate to a normal day's shooting, it also means that one dog may be very unlucky compared with another contestant. British field trials are run in four divisions: pointers and setters, German Short-haired Pointers and similar all-purpose breeds, retrievers and spaniels.

Urbanization is constantly restricting the amount of shooting for sport, but the interest in gun dog training is greater than ever before and field trials are becoming increasingly popular as a means of watching and comparing gun dogs at work.

Rabbit Hunting

The hunting group illustrated in this picture shows a basic, unchanging scene. The men are after rabbits, a type of game that seems likely to be always with us. The dogs are a mixed pack showing many of the characteristics of Ibizan Hounds. These are highly agile dogs of the greyhound type which hunt more by scent and hearing than by sight, and they are great rabbiters, either alone or in packs.

Labrador Retriever *Left*

The Labrador Retriever, both the yellow and the black, is so popular as a pet and companion that its role as a gun dog is almost forgotten. But among shooting men it is as popular as it is among pet owners. The dog's kindly nature combined with its powerful build, its excellent nose and its fondness for water, make it invaluable for retrieving game in the shooting field. Brought to England in the early nineteenth century by Labrador fishermen, the Labrador Retriever took some while to become established. Now its versatility is such that it works as a gun dog, a police dog and a guide dog for the blind, as well as being the pet of countless thousands of dog owners.

Flat-coated Retriever *Top right*

The Flat-coated Retriever has been ousted as a gun dog by the Labrador and the Golden Retriever. The reasons for this are not obvious for the Flat-coat is a handsome and industrious dog. Many rationalizations have been advanced for the changes in fortune of certain breeds but it seems likely that the very human desire for something new is all that is needed to tip the balance. The Flat-coat, which was once the favourite companion of the Victorian shooting man and his gamekeeper, is now kept only by a very few people.

Large Munsterlander *Bottom right*

Many of the German sporting breeds were decimated in the two World Wars, although the same dogs have often been taken back to their own homeland by returning servicemen, the breeds thus beginning a new life in a different area of the world. The Large Munsterlander, the descendant of the ancient German Long-haired Pointer, is still few in number. A handful of pure-bred dogs of this type were preserved in Munster-land and are now well established in Germany and beginning to be known in Britain. The colouring is the traditional one for this breed, white with black patches and black ticking.

Golden Retriever *Left*
The Golden Retriever can be any shade from richest tawny to palest cream. These handsome and popular dogs have established themselves in a triple role. In the shooting field, they are tender-mouthed and stylish workers. At the same time, together with Labradors, they are the principal breed trained to guide the blind and their reject rate, the failure of a dog to complete training, is amongst the lowest of any breed. They are also kept by an ever-increasing number of people as family pets, for their good-tempered and kindly nature makes them ideal as the friend and guardian of children.

Irish Water Spaniel *Top right*
Early writers divided spaniels into land spaniels and water spaniels. Sixteenth-century pictures of water spaniels show them to have long low-set ears and thick curly coats. Modern descendants include the Poodle and the Irish Water Spaniel. The Irish Water Spaniel is often called the clown of the spaniel family because of the contrast between its curly topknot and smooth face. It is always a rich liver colour and the coat should have crisp, tight ringlets with a natural oiliness. This is a dog with a different look but it has never caught the public fancy and its numbers are dangerously low.

Welsh Springer Spaniel *Bottom right*
Early documents suggest that a Welsh spaniel may have been known as early as 300 A.D. The name Welsh Springer did not come into use until 1902 but the dog's distinctive colouring of gleaming ice-white and brilliant chestnut red makes it easily identifiable in prints and paintings throughout the centuries. They are not, and never have been, a fashionable breed but they are in little danger of dying out as they are appreciated as general-purpose working animals in their home country. They are vigorous, keen hunters with hardy constitutions, but they also make gentle house dogs.

24

Curly-coated Retriever *Top left*
The oldest and the oddest of the retrieving breeds is the Curly-coated Retriever. The tight curls of its coat come from the water spaniel and suggest the breed's speciality is retrieving on marsh and saltflats and in river estuaries. After its Victorian heyday, it has always been a minority breed, kept going by a handful of enthusiasts. The Curly-coated Retriever has been used to retrieve duck and quail in Australia and New Zealand and has always been admired as a tender-mouthed and steady dog. Recently in Britain several have been trained as guide dogs for the blind because of their patient and reliable temperament.

English Setter *Bottom left*
The English Setter combines great physical beauty with working ability and is one of the most widely kept bird dogs in America. The long and silky coat should be slightly wavy and the white background should be flecked and freckled with either blue, orange or lemon markings. Setters range in front of the guns in order to find game, doing exactly the same job as pointers. When they scent the birds, they freeze into a point with one foreleg held up, as if to emphasize that they have been checked in mid-stride by the fabulous odour of game.

Cocker Spaniel *Right*
The popularity of the English Cocker Spaniel as a pet and companion is exceptional. It is one of the friendliest of dogs with a merry temperament and a perpetually wagging tail, which perhaps explains why it topped the popularity poll in Britain for 20 years. Its name is supposed to have come from the breed's particular proficiency in hunting woodcock, although it is little used as a gun dog today. One of the many attractions of the breed is that it comes in so many colours, including black, red, blue roan, strawberry roan and tricolour.

Gordon Setter *Top left*
As there is an Irish Setter and an English Setter, the black-and-tan Gordon Setter should really have been called the Scottish one. It is a bigger, more raw-boned dog than the other two and a methodical, dependable worker with a great deal of stamina in the field. It is mentioned by a Scottish writer in the seventeenth century as the 'black and fallow setting dog', but it was really the Fourth Duke of Richmond and Gordon who perfected the breed in the early 1800s. Most Gordons today are pets and show dogs.

Chesapeake Bay Retriever
Below left
The Chesapeake Bay Retriever is an American breed which has never achieved the popularity its reputation might suggest. It is one of a number of breeds whose speciality is retrieving wildfowl from water, especially wild duck. One of the remarkable features of the breed is its coarse, oily coat which helps it to shed water and ice simply by a good shake.

Pointer *Top right*
The Pointer is valued for its working qualities in every part of the world where people are interested in shooting game. It ranges from side to side ahead of the guns, searching for the elusive scent of the game with its extraordinarily sensitive nose. Once it has found the scent, the dog freezes like a statue, literally pointing the way. With head held high, foreleg raised as though in the act of taking a step and tail held rigid in the air, the dog will remain motionless, as if entranced, for as long as it takes the sportsmen to come up behind.

Brittany Spaniel *Bottom right*
The Brittany Spaniel is a French breed now widely used, in America as well as its country of origin, as a working gun dog. This is the only spaniel breed that 'points' to indicate the presence of game. Indeed the present dog (except for its short tail) looks very like the Elizabethan 'setting spaniel', one of the ancestors of the present-day setters. Not only is it expected to find game, it will also retrieve it when shot, being an all-round gun dog rather than a specialist.

Irish Setter *Left*

The Irish Setter is a rangier dog than the English and nowadays is almost always to be found in a rich mahogany red colour. Modern dogs are kept mainly as pets but sporting writers of a century ago remarked that they were 'slashing goers, with heads and flags well up' when they were searching for grouse on the Yorkshire moors. This is a gay dog with a headstrong, boisterous personality and it needs plenty of exercise. They were first shown in Britain in 1860 and in those days red and white Irish Setters were in the majority, the self-coloured dogs being much rarer.

German Short-haired Pointer *Right*

The German Short-haired Pointer is an all-purpose gun dog which will find game, point and retrieve the game when it has been flushed and shot. The German Short-haired is one of the most popular shooting dogs in America, although it only arrived in the States in the late 1920s. The toughness of the breed in facing heavy cover and its readiness to work in terrible weather conditions have won it many admirers. The breed has also been used by falconers to find game for birds of prey.

Clumber Spaniel *Left*
The heavyweight among the spaniels, the Clumber Spaniel is hardly ever worked in the field today. This seems to be not so much because its working abilities have declined but because the style of shooting has changed. Such a dignified, heavyweight dog is of necessity a slow worker. Pushing through dense under-growth with stubborn tenacity, the Clumber overlooks nothing in the way of game, and its stately progress through the coverts suited overweight or ageing Edwardian sportsmen. Modern shooting moves at a faster pace and the virtues of the Clumber have been forgotten.

Vizsla *Top right*
The Hungarian Vizsla is a solid-coloured dog through shades ranging from rusty gold to dark, sandy yellow. It is a powerfully built dog with a partially docked tail and a lithe, well-balanced gait. The Vizsla is a multi-purpose gun dog which points game, marks the fall of the dead bird and then retrieves it on command. In Hungary the dog is expected to work equally well whether the guns are after hares, francolin, partridge, ducks or geese. For this reason it is taught to search fairly close to the hunter on foot and not to range in the way of the English pointer.

Weimaraner *Bottom right*
Every European country produced its own version of the pointer and the Weimaraner was one of those evolved in Germany. This striking-looking dog is sometimes known as the 'grey ghost dog' as it is always mouse brown or silver grey in colour, usually with beautiful topaz or amber eyes. The breed was produced by the sportsmen nobles at the court of Weimar and later protected by a German breed club which strictly controlled breeding and ownership. An American sportsman who was admitted to this exclusive club took the breed to the States where it became an enormous success, as much as an obedience trials dog and companion as a gun dog.

Working dogs

Since man and dog first combined together as hunters, the partnership has more often than not been a working one, with man finding more and more uses for the dog as time went on. Man's superior brain has devised increasingly sophisticated applications of the dog's superior sense of hearing and smell, and the dog's superior speed, strength and stamina.

From hunting herds of grazing animals, man progressed to keeping his own domesticated flocks. One of the first domesticated animals was the reindeer and guarding and herding them was the adaptable dog. Sheepdogs can be divided into two types. There were the guard dogs, which were expected to keep off predators such as wolves. These dogs were left with the flocks, especially at night, and acted on their own initiative when danger threatened. The wild dog will defend its own territory; the domesticated dog, accepting man as the pack leader, will guard its master's belongings. Dogs like these could be left to keep the flocks in a designated area and when the sheep were moved from pasture to pasture the guard dogs led the way, rather than driving the flock from behind, the type of work done by the second type of sheepdog. The herding instinct, so strong in some working collies as to be almost a mania, is an adaptation of the hunting drives of the wild dog. Wolves driving herds of caribou will single out a weak member of the herd and kill it. The modern Border Collie working sheep shows all the movements of a hunting animal. The belly-to-the-ground crawl forward, the sudden short rush, the streaking run after a sheep that has broken away, all these are the movements of a predator stalking its prey. The fixed glare, which helps the sheepdog control the sheep and is known as showing 'eye', is paralleled by the keen, hypnotic stare of the hunting dog viewing the victim. As far as the sheepdog is concerned, it is only the final kill that is absent.

Another way in which dogs have helped man for many centuries is in the field of battle. Dogs of war were used by the Assyrians and Babylonians, and the invading Romans were much impressed by the fighting strength of the British Mastiff. Early Irish literature mentions that Wolfhounds accompanied their masters into battle and were large and strong enough to pull the enemy from his horse. Modern Army and Air Force dogs no longer have this offensive role; instead they are used in the role of communications. They lay telephone cables and carry messages, being trained to run to and fro between two masters. Army dogs are used for mine detection as they can scent buried mines from a distance. Trained mine-detecting dogs save both time and manpower. The Air Force uses trained dogs to find the missing parts of crashed planes. Air Force dogs are also used as the most efficient way of guarding aerodromes. The dogs' acute hearing and their ability to pick up windborne scents mean that they can detect intruders hundreds of yards away. When Air Force dogs detect an intruder on an airfield, they may be loosed to detain the trespasser until the arrival of their handler. Army patrol dogs, however, which are used in guerrilla warfare to detect the presence of the enemy, must not give away their position by approaching a suspected ambush or by barking or growling. When they pick up an alien scent that may indicate danger, they are trained to freeze or point like a gun dog scenting game. During the Second World War, rescue dogs were parachuted down with stretcher bearers of the airborne divisions.

The dog's scenting powers have been used in many ways. The Italians still use dogs to hunt truffles, that elusive and expensive underground fungi. Gas companies use dogs to search for gas leaks, thus saving the expense of digging up a whole pipeline. Police and customs' dogs are trained to search for drugs. There are mountain rescue dog teams which will search for lost climbers and there are avalanche rescue dogs which will indicate where people are buried, in much the same way as a sheepdog will guide the shepherd to sheep buried in snowdrifts.

Dogs have been used extensively as pack animals. The explorer Marco Polo remarked on the sledges drawn by mastiff-like dogs in Manchuria, and sledge dogs once provided the only means of transport for all the peoples inhabiting the frozen wastes of Alaska, Greenland and Siberia. These dogs endured lives of incredible hardship, for, although they were highly valued and well looked after by their owners, the conditions under which they lived and worked were such that only the fittest and toughest could survive. Farm dogs in Europe were once used as draught dogs, pulling loads of bread, cork, olives, wine, baskets and cheeses. Pack dogs carrying food and ammunition have accompanied hunters in the field and dogs took shells forward to the guns in the First World War. Today draught dogs are diminishing rapidly in numbers everywhere in the world as their role is taken over by the internal combustion engine. But as one kind of work disappears dogs become useful in other ways, for instance, in medical and space research or for guiding the blind.

Border Collie

The Border Collie is the most versatile and widely kept working sheepdog in the world. As they have been selected for their working abilities for many generations, the instinct to herd is inborn in most Border Collies and quite young puppies will attempt to round up any animals they come across, such as hens or ducks. Because of this built-in drive to work, they are often too highly strung to make satisfactory pets, being much happier if given a job of work to do. Highly intelligent and sensitive, the Border Collie is often used by competitors in obedience tests with great success.

Guide Dog for the Blind *Left*
One of the most responsible jobs a dog can have is guiding a blind owner. The organization that trains these dogs looks for animals of medium size, as the giant breeds are too big for comfortable working and too costly to maintain. The dogs must have a stable temperament, neither nervous nor aggressive. They must be willing to please and have a high degree of concentration. In practice the most common breeds chosen are Labradors and Golden Retrievers. Here a Yellow Labrador takes her owner to work.

Pyrenean Mountain Dog *Top right*
The Pyrenean Mountain Dog or Great Pyrenees used to guard flocks of sheep from wolves and other predators in the isolated mountain areas of France. By the seventeenth century it had become a fashionable dog in aristocratic French circles and guarded many of the chateaux of south-west France. The beautiful coat and impressive size make the Pyrenean a very attractive dog, but it needs adequate space, a great deal of food, and time spent on daily grooming if it is to be seen at its best.

Doberman Pinscher *Bottom right*
The Doberman is used as a police and Army dog, particularly in the United States, and has the reputation of having a very suspicious nature and very quick reactions. This breed was the creation of one man, Louis Dobermann, who wanted a guard dog *par excellence*. In the 1870s, in Germany, he crossed a number of local breeds to get the type he wanted. Since then some of the ferocity which made the breed noted in its early years has been bred out and the Doberman is now a stable, intelligent dog as well as a first-class guard dog.

Sled Dog

The Arctic Sled Dog, for so long the only means of transport in that region, must be among the toughest of all working animals. The Eskimos use them for haulage and hunting, for warmth and for food when times are very bad. The dogs are accustomed to feeding on frozen scraps and to sleeping in hollows which they scrape in the frozen surface of the tundra. Blizzards often cover them with drifted snow but, insulated by their thick coats, they can sleep out the worst of storms. Various methods of harnessing are used but the most popular is couples of dogs fastened on either side of a trace going out to the team leader.

Komondor *Top right*

The Komondor is the largest of the sheep and cattle working dogs of Hungary and is primarily a guard dog left to watch the herds and protect them. This is a position of trust where much is left to the dog's initiative. Like many pastoral guard dogs, the Komondor is white, perhaps so that it can be seen more easily at night. The tremendous coat falls in matted cords forming an almost impenetrable mass which protects the dog against the weather and any injury. A truly impressive dog, the bigger the Komondor is the better.

Bearded Collie *Bottom right*

The raggle-taggle charm of the Bearded Collie has only recently been appreciated. The breed, used for working both sheep and cattle in the Scottish hills, was not recognized as pure-bred until 1948, when the first one was registered with the Kennel Club. They are active dogs, racily built under a weather-resistant shaggy coat which insulates them from cold and wet. Their love of life, their curiosity and their desire to please make them excellent family pets for those who want an intelligent and energetic dog.

38

Labrador Retriever *Left*
The latest recruit in the battle against drug-smuggling is the Labrador Retriever. Police officers and customs officials are beginning to appreciate the worth of a trained dog whose nose can find hidden cargoes which might be missed even after a laborious and time-consuming search. It takes some months to train a dog in drug detection and such an animal is considered a specialist and relieved from other police duties. Drugs can be detected by the dogs even when in closed, sealed canisters. This Yellow Labrador is searching for cannabis.

German Shepherd *Right*
The German Shepherd is the dog used most widely by police forces throughout the world. Their high degree of trainability plus their agility and strength make them an ideal choice as police and Army dogs. Attacking on command is only one of the many facets of the work they are trained for, although it is probably the one with the most news value. Police work demands reliability and steadiness of nerve and a well-trained German Shepherd has both. Because they are very intelligent, they are happiest as working companions and can become dangerously aggressive if allowed to get bored. In England, police dogs live at home with their trainers as part of the family so that a complete relationship can be established. Outside the police force, German Shepherds are popular guard dogs and they are also trained as guide dogs for the blind.

40

Siberian Husky *Left*

As Eskimo settlements are invariably isolated, a number of distinct types of husky were evolved. Many of these breeds were lost during the Alaska gold rush when every dog, whatever its shape and size, was pressed into service to haul prospectors and their supplies to the gold fields. One breed that did survive was the Siberian Husky. This is a comparatively lightweight haulage dog, well known through the popularity of the sport of sled dog racing. Many Siberians are shown and kept as companions, and they adapt well to a temperate climate. The light blue eyes are quite common in this breed.

Briard and Old English Sheepdog *Top right*

The black Briard is a French sheepdog and the slate and white Old English Sheepdog comes from Britain. The similarities between the two breeds indicate that they are both descended from a very old race of shaggy sheepdogs probably brought to Europe by early Asian invaders. The Briard, a long-tailed dog which can also be fawn in colour, still guards French farmsteads and has a distinguished record as an Army and Red Cross dog. The Old English Sheepdog, nicknamed 'Bobtail' because of its short docked tail, is now only a show dog and companion.

Mastiff *Bottom right*

One of the largest and heaviest of all breeds, the Mastiff was also one of Britain's first exports. The invading Romans, under the leadership of Julius Caesar, were so impressed by the British dogs fighting alongside their masters that they sent some to Rome to take part in the gladiatorial games. Sadly, breeding stock in Britain did not survive the Second World War and Mastiffs would have become extinct in their native land had American owners not supplied further specimens. This must be the most impressive of guard dogs for those with the money for its upkeep.

42

Puli *Top left*
The Puli, smaller and darker-coloured than the Komondor, was used in Hungary to drive and herd sheep during the day. This is a sprightly dog with a springy gait and plenty of vigour and intelligence, which has led to the breed being used for police work in Hungary and obedience work in the States. The coat can be combed out, but the cords are a distinctive feature of the breed. The long strands of the outer coat twist round the soft, easily matted undercoat, forming a felted mass. The dog can be bathed without disturbing the corded appearance.

Welsh Corgi *Bottom left*
Both the Welsh Corgis, the Pembroke and the Cardigan, were originally cattle drover's dogs. Before the advent of the railways, cattle were driven long distances from farm to slaughter house and cattle dogs were essential to move the herds. The short legs of the Corgi breeds enabled them to race in and nip the heels of recalcitrant beasts while dodging the flailing hooves. The more popular Pembroke Corgi shown here is the smaller of the two and has a short docked tail. The Cardigan Corgi has a long tail like a fox's brush.

Rough Collie *Right*
This strikingly elegant breed no longer works as a sheepdog, its place among the flocks having been taken over by the Border Collie. In fact both these dogs probably came from the same ancestral root, the hard-working rough-coated shepherd's dog of the Scottish hills. In the early 1800s Queen Victoria popularized the Rough Collie, which rapidly became a favourite on both sides of the Atlantic. More chic and sophisticated in appearance than its country cousins, the Rough Collie still retains the willing desire to please of a working dog.

44

Kelpie *Left*
The Kelpie is the working sheepdog of Australia where it is reckoned that one Kelpie can do the work of six men. This is a compact, tough dog capable of covering 40-45 miles (65-70 kilometres) a day. Used to dealing with vast numbers of sheep, the dogs often work out of sight of the stockmen. Where the sheep are penned in large numbers, as in the sheep sale yards, the Kelpie will run over the backs of the tightly packed flocks to reach a certain position. The Kelpie is an extremely popular breed in Australia where it is shown as well as worked, but the dog is almost unknown outside its homeland.

Australian Cattle Dog *Top right*
The Australian Cattle Dog is a working breed superbly adapted for a specific job — that of driving, rounding up and penning range cattle. The steers are virtually wild and the dogs have to be tough individualists prepared to bite hard and get out of the way fast. They are agile and rugged, able to work in the heat and drive herds for trips covering many hundreds of miles. They are normally blue or mottled blue in colour, probably a legacy from the Smooth Collie in their ancestry.

Great Dane *Bottom right*
The Great Dane is remarkable for its size, being very muscular and strong and at the same time elegantly built. Despite its name, this dog is a native of Germany where it was used to hunt wild boar. The best modern Danes are to be found in the United States, as two World Wars have lowered breed standards elsewhere. Acceptable colours include fawn, brindle, black, blue and harlequin (white with black patches).

Hunting dogs

Hounds fall basically into two categories, those that hunt by sight and those that hunt by scent. Those that hunt by sight are the greyhounds, sometimes called the gazehounds. They include such breeds as the Saluki, the Afghan Hound, the Borzoi or Russian Wolfhound, and the Deerhound. All these hounds have been bred for speed so that they can overtake the swiftest and most agile of quarry. It is easy to see the likeness between them. They have tall, elongated bodies with long powerful limbs. The back is long and arched so that it can act as a powerful spring when the dog gallops. The long strong tail acts as an efficient rudder so that the dog can turn and twist at speed. The depth of the rib cage ensures plenty of heart and lung room, and the dog carries no superfluous flesh or fat.

The dogs run mute, needing all their breath for galloping. Once its quarry is out of sight, the greyhound gives up. These dogs are therefore specifically suited to hunting in open country. They have been used on the Russian steppes to pull down wolves and in the sandy wastes of Persia to hunt gazelle and desert foxes. They have hunted antelope on the plains of the Orient and deer and hares on the moors and mountainsides of Britain. They are seen at their best in the unenclosed, uninterrupted spaces of the world and as these get fewer and fewer there is less and less for the coursing hounds to hunt.

Many of these breeds are now kept solely as pets by people who admire their elegance and grace. The thrill of coursing live game across open country, which was enjoyed by so many of our ancestors, has now been replaced by the thrills of greyhound racing. This is the biggest of all modern dog businesses, and each year many thousands of dogs are registered with the appropriate governing body of the sport. Not only are winning dogs very valuable in their own right, a considerable amount of money is gambled on greyhound racing. The idea of dogs chasing a mechanically propelled artificial hare was tried out in Britain in the 1870s and failed. It was revived in the 1920s in the U.S.A. with a circular track and an electrically controlled hare. The sport very rapidly became popular throughout the States and was brought back to Britain a few years later.

The second category of hounds are those that hunt by scent. They are generally not as swift as greyhounds for they do not need to keep their quarry in sight. Following the scent of their quarry, they can take a more leisurely pace, wearing the game down by persistence and endurance. These hounds are more diverse in shape than the greyhounds, and can vary from a low-legged animal like the Dachshund to a large powerful beast like the Bloodhound. They rely almost entirely on their noses for hunting and use their eyes and ears very little. They very often have long pendent ears, full of folds, which hang down over the eyes when the dog is tracking. Unlike greyhounds, these dogs do not run mute. The cry of the Bloodhound indicates not only the nature of the quarry but also the direction in which it is moving and how far it is ahead of the pack.

Hounds are used in many different ways in many different countries. They are often used by shooting men to find game and may be expected to retrieve it when it is shot. In some parts of the world, hounds are trained to work round behind game and drive it towards the guns. The greatest variety of hounds is probably to be found in France, although hunting by packs of hounds barely survived the French Revolution. In Britain the number of packs of hounds has steadily increased during the twentieth century. Most packs are foxhounds which are hunted on horseback, but there are also a number of beagle and basset hound packs which are followed on foot. There are also a few trail hounds which race round the fell country in the north of England following an aniseed trail laid for them.

By far the greatest number of hounds in the modern world is in America, where there are reckoned to be well over one and a half million. Over the centuries the very best English and French hound blood has been imported into the States, although few of these dogs have been hunted in packs in the European style. The American Foxhound can be used in a variety of ways and for this reason alone type is not very uniform. The field trial hound, which is run competitively at field trials, has to be speedy and has a rather jealous nature. The foxhound used by the sportsman who hunts the fox with a gun is a slow trailing hound with a good voice. The trail or drag hounds which race along a specially laid trail need speed and stamina alone. American Foxhounds are hunted in packs which are followed on horseback, although their quarry need not necessarily be a fox.

Another extremely popular hound in America is the Coonhound, of which there are some six varieties. As their name suggests, they are bred to hunt racoons. The owner looses the dog at night in forest or swamp land and the hound casts silently around until it picks up a trail. It bays whilst it is following the scent, and when the racoon climbs a tree the dog remains baying at the foot of the tree until the hunter arrives.

Foxhound

Fox-hunting dates from about the middle of the eighteenth century, although packs of hounds have existed since man first became a hunter. Earlier hound packs hunted wild boar, wolves and deer, but as the countryside became more settled and enclosed the larger animals of the chase became extinct and the fox, whose numbers had to be controlled, became the main object of the hunt. Packs of hounds have probably been bred with more care and thought over the centuries than most other animals and the result is a compact, powerful animal of tremendous stamina and scenting power.

Borzoi *Left*
The alternative name for the Borzoi — Russian Wolfhound — gives a clue to the breed's origins. One of the favourite sports of the Imperial Court of the Russian Empire was coursing the wolf. The Czars and the Russian nobility kept enormous numbers of hounds with which to indulge their taste for a rather formalized type of hunting where hounds were loosed in pairs to bring wolves to bay. The Russian Revolution would have ended the breed as such had it not already been established in Britain and the United States by the end of the nineteenth century.

Jack Russell Terrier *Top right*
Though not a pedigree dog nor officially recognized as a breed by the Kennel Club, the Jack Russell is firmly established as a pet in Britain. Jaunty, sporting little dogs with a game and independent character, their low-legged build and small size mean that they adapt equally well to urban or country life. Named after a nineteenth-century parson, who was also a founder member of the Kennel Club, it is unlikely that the present-day Jack Russell bears much resemblance to the terriers kept by this Devon vicar.

Cairn Terrier *Bottom right*
The Cairn Terrier is another Scottish breed which lacks a well-documented history. It was used in western Scotland to tackle all vermin from rats to wild cats and therefore did not move in the sort of company where its history was likely to be written down. A cheeky little dog with a shaggy coat that needs little in the way of attention, the Cairn is one of the most popular terriers in Britain and well established in America, Australia and on the Continent. Its gay and lively disposition makes it a cheerful companion.

Dachshund *Left*
These long, low-to-the-ground dogs are German in origin and were bred to go underground after badgers. Their shape enabled them to follow the tunnels of the badger's set where they were meant to keep the occupant at bay until it could be dug out and despatched. The dog's loud ringing bark helped the gamekeeper to locate their position underground. Now kept only as pets, Dachshunds come in three different coat varieties: long-haired, smooth-haired and wire-haired. Miniature Dachshunds must weigh under 11 lb (5 kg).

Basenji *Top right*
The Basenji is one of the oldest hunting dogs and was well known to the Pharaohs of ancient Egypt. This is a lightly built dog with a gazelle-like grace, distinctive pricked ears, a tightly curled tail and wrinkled forehead. Recently rediscovered by Europeans in the Congo, Basenjis were used there to hunt all the smaller types of equatorial game. Running mute, the dogs had wooden bells hung round their necks so that their native owners could track them when they were hidden by the tall elephant grass. They are unusual in that they do not bark, making chortling and yodelling noises instead.

Otterhound *Bottom right*
In the United States a number of Otterhounds are exhibited at dog shows, although their numbers are relatively few. In Britain there is only one pure-bred pack and it is obviously a breed that is in grave danger of disappearing altogether. Otterhounds are rather like Bloodhounds in appearance, except for their hard wiry coats, and they have the same remarkable scenting powers. They are handsome dogs, very hardy and excellent swimmers but they seem unlikely to survive in a world increasingly concerned with the conservation of the rarer wild animals, including the otter.

Afghan Hound *Top left*
One of the most beautiful and spectacular of breeds, the Afghan is very popular as a pet. Originally kept in Afghanistan for hunting such animals as gazelle and desert fox, the Afghan has no equal for negotiating uneven ground at speed. The powerful loins, wide-set hip bones and large padded feet all help the dog to turn easily without slowing its pace. The long, silky coat can be almost any colour. Dogs built for speed like this one need plenty of exercise and time must also be set aside for daily grooming.

Deerhound *Bottom.left*
This dog has a history so closely interwoven with that of Scotland that it might almost be called the national breed. A powerful and dignified animal, the appearance of the Deerhound has altered little over the last 150 years, although their numbers have fluctuated alarmingly during that period. Originally the hounds were bred for strength and stamina to overtake wounded stags and bring them to bay. With the development of the sporting rifle, the need for such hounds grew less and their numbers subsequently declined. They are now kept by the discerning few who appreciate the dog's dignity and devotion.

Basset Hound *Right*
The Basset Hound is another hunting dog which is better known nowadays by the fireside than in the field. Heavily boned, short-legged hounds like these were once used on the Continent to hunt everything from deer to wild boar. Modern Basset packs hunt the hare and are followed on foot. They are known for their remarkable scenting power and perseverance, rather than their speed. As pets it should be remembered that these are large dogs on short legs which require good feeding and plenty of exercise.

Fox Terrier *Top left*
Nearly all the terriers were used to attack vermin such as rats, rabbits and foxes. Rather than hunt them across country, the terrier's job was to follow their prey underground and hold them there until help arrived. The Fox Terrier, which can have either a smooth or wire-haired coat, used to run with the hounds and came into its own when the fox went to earth. The much-barbered look of the Wire-haired Fox Terrier shown here may have something to do with its present decline from popularity.

Whippet *Bottom left*
The Whippet has aptly been described as 'one of the most graceful running machines in existence'. The breed was created in the north of England during the latter half of the nineteenth century for the sport of rabbit coursing. When this became illegal, rag racing took its place. The dogs were encouraged to swing and pull on a rag held by their owners and would race towards this entrancing object flapping at the end of the track. Today Whippets are mainly kept as pets.

Greyhound Racing *Top right*
When it was first staged in the 1870s greyhound racing was a failure, but it became an enormous money-spinning success when revived at floodlit evening meetings in the United States and Britain during the 1920s. Greyhounds are the fastest dogs in the world, reaching more than 37 miles (59 km) an hour over short distances. They hunt entirely by sight and race after a mechanically propelled hare. They wear light cage-type muzzles when racing to prevent them snapping at each other in the excitement of the melee after they have crossed the finishing line.

Elkhound *Bottom right*
The Norwegian Elkhound has a claim to be one of the oldest breeds in Europe. They are dogs of endurance and stamina whose role throughout thousands of years has been to guard the home and the domestic flocks, and to co-operate with man in hunting large quarry such as bear and reindeer, as well as elk. The hounds, working alone or in pairs, were expected to locate and hold at bay these large animals until the hunters could reach the spot.

Bloodhound *Left*
The Bloodhound must qualify as the dog with the most mournful face, but despite the melancholy expression and the spine-chilling name they are usually gentle and kindly beasts. They hunt by scent and their skill for this is legendary. In the past they have been used to hunt runaway slaves, find missing persons and track down wanted criminals. Bloodhound enthusiasts still arrange hunts, a runner being sent ahead to lay a trail for the hounds to follow. The sound of their sonorous baying when following a line is said to be the most unforgettable of all hound music.

Lakeland Terrier *Top right*
The Lakeland Terrier, as its name suggests, comes from the fell country in the north of England. These terriers accompanied the packs of fell hounds and went to ground after foxes. There are many stories of them being lost underground for days at a time before being rescued unhurt and still courageous and undaunted. The dog has a well-balanced head with powerful jaws, and its narrow body enables it to wriggle through rock fissures and crannies. The modern show dog has the dense wiry coat thinned out to smarten its appearance but at heart it is still a game working dog.

Saluki *Bottom right*
A graceful and attractive dog looking very like the Saluki has been portrayed on Assyrian and Babylonian bas-reliefs, on Classical Greek vases and in Renaissance oil paintings and tapestries. They have been known round the Mediterranean throughout history and were the favourite hounds of the nomadic desert sheiks who used them for hunting gazelle, often in partnership with falcons. So favoured a dog were they that they are said to be the only ones the Arabs would allow in their tents, the rest of the canine race being considered unclean.

58

Pharaoh Hound *Left*

The Pharaoh Hound is the same type of greyhound as those depicted in the murals of ancient Egypt. The dog has a lithe, lean build and an approximately square outline when seen from the side. As well as being speedy and agile, Pharaoh Hounds are phenomenal jumpers. They are used for hunting rabbits, which they do more like a lurcher than a greyhound, for they use scent and hearing to a greater degree than sight. The large upstanding ears are a feature of the breed.

Beagle *Top right*

The modern Beagle is known in a dual role. As merry and active animals of a handy size for urban life, they are deservedly popular as pets both in the United States and Britain. As pack dogs used for hunting the hare, they have a much more ancient history. From Roman times to the modern day, Beagle packs have attracted an enthusiastic following. As they are followed on foot and not on horseback, this is an energetic sport. Part of the charm of the pet Beagle is this close sporting background.

Irish Wolfhound *Bottom right*

The Irish Wolfhound is the heavy-weight and the tallest amongst the hounds. There are many references in early Irish literature to these majestic dogs, which were always highly prized and frequently sent as gifts by local chieftains. When wolves became extinct in Ireland, the Wolfhound also declined in number, only to be revived in the nineteenth century. It seems very fitting that this dignified and noble dog should be the mascot of the Irish Guards regiment.

Family life

Puppies are born relatively undeveloped and helpless. This means that a bitch has to show a fairly high degree of maternal care if the litter is to survive. Her instinct is to give birth in a safe, secluded den and there are many instances of dogs digging their own burrows before giving birth. Farm dogs, for example, will tunnel into haystacks to make a warm, insulated den. The best kind of whelping box, therefore, is one which is low enough for the mother just to be able to stand and the door of the box just big enough for her to get through. This enclosed space will satisfy the bitch's need for safety, seclusion and darkness. The floor space should be large enough for her to stretch out flat on her side. The box should also have a removable top so that the puppies can be looked at and reached if anything goes wrong.

All puppies, whatever their breed, look very much the same at birth. They are blind and deaf and covered with short sleek fur. Their muzzles are blunt and their ears folded and crumpled. Their legs seem too small for their bodies and cannot yet support the puppy's weight. There are differences in birth weights between breeds, of course, but these are not so great as the differences in size of the adult dogs might lead one to expect. A puppy of a toy breed might weigh 4 oz (113 g) at birth and grow up to be a 6-lb (2.72-kg) adult, thus increasing its body weight 24 times. A puppy of a much larger breed might well weigh 2 lb (907 g) when born and weigh 100 lb (45.4 kg) when adult, an increase of 50 times. This is one of the reasons why large breeds are slower to develop and mature. The small dog may be fully grown by 8 months but one of the giant breeds will not be mature until 2½ or 3 years of age. Because big dogs need extra food for growth over such a long time, they are even more expensive to keep than many people realize.

Two things are vital for very young puppies and these are food and warmth. All animals have methods to keep their body temperature constant even though the temperature of their surroundings may alter, but for the first few days of their lives puppies have not yet developed this ability to keep themselves warm. At this stage they are more like reptiles and their body temperature varies according to the temperature of their surroundings. The only way a puppy can remain warm is by maintaining constant contact with its mother. Her instinct is to remain with her newborn litter and she cannot normally be persuaded to leave them for more than a minute or two.

Puppies who cannot find their mother to snuggle close to begin to cry and crawl round in circles. If for some reason their distress calls do not bring the mother back, their movements get slower and slower as they get colder and colder. At the same time, all their bodily functions begin to slow down. The heart does not beat as fast and they cannot digest any food they may be given. Paradoxically this cataleptic state may be an asset to survival in the wild where puppies which were noisy and active during their mother's absence might well attract the attention of predators.

Puppies are born with the so-called 'rooting reflex'. This causes the puppy to push towards a teat almost as soon as it is born. It will burrow under other members of the litter, showing a surprising amount of strength and persistence. The tongue of a young puppy is curved like a scoop, making a very efficient sucking mechanism. While the puppies are feeding, they also knead the mother's milk glands with their front paws to stimulate the supply.

Most puppies open their eyes between the tenth and fourteenth day of life. Like kittens and most human babies their eyes are blue and do not function very well at first. By the eighth or ninth week they will have darkened to the adult colour. During the third week the puppies begin to hear and to show interest in their litter mates and in people. They learn to wag their tails and their legs are now strong enough to support their body weight.

The puppies begin to bark and growl and to attempt to play with each other and with their mother. The instinct to keep the nest clean is inborn and as soon as the puppy can walk it will move away from the sleeping area before relieving itself. This instinct to keep the place where it lives reasonably clean is the one we want to foster when we housetrain a puppy.

Mock fighting begins at this stage among the members of the litter and this establishes which puppy will be leader of the group. Normally the biggest male tends to become the leader, as in the wild, but in a litter of bitch puppies it is often the noisiest female. The mother disciplines the litter, growling and nipping if they pester her unduly or are too rough in their play. This also is very important for the puppies' development and there is evidence to suggest that if, for any reason, a puppy misses this period of play with its litter mates and its mother, it may never have a normal relationship with other dogs when it is adult. It may become a life-long bully or a coward. It is at this stage too that puppies must have human contact for the man/dog relationship to become fixed. This association must take place between the third and fifth week of the puppy's life. Once the bond has been established by contact at this critical period in the puppy's life, it can never be entirely broken.

Smooth Fox Terrier
A Smooth Fox Terrier bitch and her puppies enjoy a meal, although some of the puppies do not look very interested. The Smooth Fox Terrier has never become fashionable, unlike its cousin the Wire-haired Fox Terrier. The difference between the two lies in the coat rather than the structure, and in the nineteenth century, when most were still kept for killing stable rats, they were bred together indiscriminately. A smart, uncomplicated, hard-bitten little dog, the Smooth Fox Terrier will always have its admirers.

West Highland White *Left*
These newly born West Highland White puppies are snuggling up to their proud mother for food and warmth. Bitches should never be left to whelp on their own in case there are complications which might require veterinary assistance. Here the owner has dried the puppy on a towel before giving it back. Puppies are born relatively undeveloped, being unable to see, hear or stand. However different they will be when adult, newly born puppies all look much the same with folded ears, eyes shut and short blunt muzzles.

Spitz *Top right*
Dogs of Spitz type like this one are the working dogs of the northern latitudes. This group of dogs all have wedge-shaped heads with blunt powerful jaws and small pricked ears. The bushy tail is usually curled up over the back and the dense coat offers a complete protection against the harshest winter weather. All the sled dogs are of this type and so are a number of other northern breeds. This Norwegian farm dog suckles her litter in between her work, which can be anything from driving the cows out to pasture, accompanying the farmer out shooting or guarding the farmyard against human or animal intruders.

West Highland White *Bottom right*
This is the same West Highland White litter, eight weeks later and fully weaned. Their mother may want to visit them for periods of play but she will no longer feed or sleep with the puppies. 'Westies' are now the most popular terrier in Britain and are widely kept and shown in America. They have the advantage of being very natural dogs, with a light-hearted and plucky temperament. West Highland Whites come from the same root as Scottish Terriers and Cairn Terriers and the breed has inherited the hardiness of its vermin-killing ancestors. Although the coat is white, it is harsh in texture and easily sheds dirt.

Dogs and Cats *Left*
Animosity between dogs and cats is often an attitude fostered primarily by their owners. The two species can in fact live very happily together, enjoying each other's company. Playing seems to be as essential for young animals as it is for young humans. Mock attacks strengthen muscles and reflexes and in many of the actions can be seen the shadow play of the kill which, as predators, these puppies would have to make for survival in the wild. In introducing a new puppy or kitten into a household where there is already an established pet, care should be taken to keep the causes of jealousy to a minimum.

St Bernard *Top right*
Large dogs tend to have large litters and it would not be unusual for St Bernards like these to have ten or more puppies in a litter. Feeding so many puppies is a very expensive business and their diet has to be more than adequate to maintain the necessary growth rate. Dogs like these have massive bones, and calcium and vitamin supplements are even more essential than usual. The average adult male St Bernard will weigh about 180 lb (81.6 kg), and the highest recorded weight for one of the breed is 259 lb (117.5 kg). These puppies have got a great deal more growing to do to match that.

Basset Hound *Bottom right*
If possible, puppies should be fed from separate dishes, so that they can all be sure of a fair share instead of the weakest and less determined ones being kept back. The puppies shown feeding here are Basset Hound puppies. Recent advertising campaigns using these dogs have helped to popularize them as pets. When breeds suddenly become well known in this way and desirable as status symbols, it is not always to the dog's advantage. Bassets are large, low-to-the-ground sporting dogs which need a lot of exercise and many of their new owners do not appreciate this.

66

Beagle *Top left*
Puppies need space to run and play in, and without it they cannot develop as well as they should. Puppies kept in minute pens under insanitary conditions cannot follow their instincts to keep their bed and immediate surroundings clean, and this can lead to house-training problems later. Although Beagles are mainly kept today as pets rather than as hunting dogs, this Beagle family still needs plenty of exercise.

Sealyham Terrier *Bottom left*
These pups with their long-suffering mother are young Sealyham Terriers. It remains a mystery why one short-legged white terrier, the West Highland White, should be so popular, while the other short-legged white terrier, the Sealyham, can scarcely muster a tenth of its numbers. Sealyhams got their name from a country estate in Wales where over a hundred years ago an eccentric sportsman bred his own terriers for dealing with otters and polecats. Since then the Sealyham has been smartened up in appearance and the somewhat foolhardy temperament has been toned down to reasonable proportions. Often comical characters, their devotees claim the breed has a good sense of humour.

Poodle *Right*
Most dogs, like most children, like to show off. Teaching your dog games and tricks will give you both a lot of fun. The best games use the dog's natural abilities to the full, for example, teaching it to use its nose to search for hidden objects. The best tricks are those which develop from things your dog does naturally. Bouncy dogs can show off by jumping to command, and some small dogs quite often walk on their hindlegs when they want to see higher and further. Even the heavyweight, non-athletic breeds can be taught to shake hands or 'die for their country'.

Bearded Collie *Top left*
Changes of coat colour as a dog grows older are often dramatic and not always entirely predictable. This dark brown Bearded Collie puppy may end up as light a shade as its mother when its adult coat finally comes through. All Old English Sheepdogs are born black and white and only become grey or grizzled later in life. Liver Bedlington Terriers are born dark brown and change to a light biscuit shade. Even the spots on the Dalmatian are not there at birth, only beginning to appear as dark smudges at about three weeks.

Pointer *Bottom left*
A litter of eight puppies is as much as any bitch should be asked to rear. In a number of continental countries where specialist clubs control the breeding of pedigree animals very strictly, six puppies is considered to be the maximum that should be left in a litter. Not only should the mother have unlimited good food, the puppies themselves may need supplementary feeding as well as extra-early weaning. Pointers like this one are a very fertile breed which often has large litters.

Golden Retriever *Top right*
From the moment of birth, puppies are the most ruthless egoists. These week-old Golden Retriever puppies are still deaf and blind, for their eyes and ears will not function until they are 10 to 12 days old. All puppies, however, are born with the rooting reflex which ensures that they nuzzle towards a teat for the all-important life-giving milk within minutes of birth. The favoured position is under the mother's hind leg where there is warmth and where the milk supply is more abundant. The strongest puppies will always be found in this position.

Labrador *Bottom right*
Like all young animals, puppies need plenty of uninterrupted sleep if they are to grow and flourish. Healthy puppies are either eating, playing or utterly relaxed in the appealing sleep of babyhood. This exhausted Yellow Labrador mother snoozes beside her puppies, although at this stage the bitch often likes to get a little peace by sleeping away from the litter. A floor covering of newspaper is the most economical for puppies reared indoors, as it can be changed at frequent intervals.

Acknowledgements

The publishers would like to thank the following for their kind permission to reproduce the pictures in this book.

AFA 1
Animal Photography 2-3, 5, 7 below, 9 above, 9 below, 10 above, 12, 16 above, 16 below, 19 below, 22, 23 above, 24, 25 above, 26 above, 26 below, 28 above, 29 above, 29 below, 32, 33 above, 37 below, 39 below, 44 above, 47 above, 50, 51 above, 53 above, 54 above, 57 below, 59 above, 59 below, 69, 70 above, front and back flaps
Aspect (Derek Bayes) 28 below
Anne Cumbers 8, 17 below, 25 below, 27, 35, 37 above, 39 above, 42, 43 above, 43 below, 51 below, 54 below, 56 above, 61 below, 63, 64, 65 below, 70 below, 71 above, 71 below
Christopher Davies 10 below
Thomas Fall 19 above
The Guide Dogs for the Blind Association 36
Claire Leimbach 47 below
Chris Maresch 6, 46
Jim Meads 49, 53 below, 55, 58, 61 above
John Moss 7 above, 13 below, 15 above, 17 above, 30, 40, 44 below, 56 below, 60, 68 above
Pictor 72
Spectrum 14, 15 below, 52, 66, 68 below
Tony Stone 18, 33 below, 45, front jacket
Syndication International 67 below
Z.E.F.A. E. Deyle - 21 and back jacket, D. Grathwohl - 23 below, W. L. Hamilton - 57 above, E. Hummel - 38, Puck/Korneztski - 11, M. Nissen - 13 above, E. Oechstein - 41, Walter Schmidt - 65 above, H. G. Trenkwalder - 67 above